North Walsham

in old picture postcards

by
Mary McManus, Ron Fiske and Michael Ling
for the North Walsham & District Historical Society

Second edition

European Library - Zaltbommel/Netherlands MCMLXXXV

We are most grateful to the many people who have loaned items and helped in the production of this book.

GB   ISBN 90 288 3116 9 / CIP

European Library in Zaltbommel/Netherlands publishes among other things the following series:

IN OLD PICTURE POSTCARDS *is a series of books which sets out to show what a particular place looked like and what life was like in Victorian and Edwardian times. A book about virtually every town in the United Kingdom is to be published in this series. By the end of this year about 175 different volumes will have appeared. 1,250 books have already been published devoted to the Netherlands with the title* **In oude ansichten.** *In Germany, Austria and Switzerland 500, 60 and 15 books have been published as* **In alten Ansichten;** *in France by the name* **En cartes postales anciennes** *and in Belgium as* **En cartes postales anciennes** *and/or* **In oude prentkaarten** *150 respectively 400 volumes have been published.*

For further particulars about published or forthcoming books, apply to your bookseller or direct to the publisher.

This edition has been printed and bound by Grafisch Bedrijf De Steigerpoort in Zaltbommel/Netherlands.

INTRODUCTION

North Walsham is probably one of the most conveniently situated market towns in Norfolk. This is a quotation from an old guide book to the town and it is still true. The town stands on comparatively high ground between the River Ant on the east and the River Bure on the west, five miles from the coast, within easy reach of the Norfolk Broads and sixteen miles from Norwich, the county town.

Traces of Roman occupation were found in 1844 when Roman coins, urns and bronze figures were discovered to the west of the town on Felmingham Heath. Many of these objects are now in the British Museum.

North Walsham began as a Saxon settlement, the home of Wael or Walsa, and developed as a trading centre of the surrounding countryside. That the Vikings also had a settlement here is proved by the fact that a Norseman named Sket gave the town and its church to the Cluniac Abbey of St. Benet about seven miles away.

Mention is made in Domesday Book of a church at Walsam, as it was then called, with thirty acres of land belonging to it. When Edward III brought Flemish weavers to England in the twelfth century to improve the standard of English weaving, some of them settled at Worstead, three miles south-east of North Walsham, and the place eventually gave its name to a woollen material now known as 'Worsted'.

North Walsham and the surrounding villages were all occupied in the production of woollen cloth in their homes and a new Wool Hall for the storing and marketing of the material in the town is mentioned in a record of 1391. There was a fabric known as Walsham Cloth.

In the thirteenth century, the town was granted a charter to hold a market every Thursday by Henry III when he passed through on one of his visits to Bacton to venerate the Holy Rood of Bromholm which was reputed to be a portion of the cross on which Christ died and to have miraculous powers of healing and for which Bromholm Priory was celebrated. A market is still held every Thursday in the Market Place in the centre of the town.

The Black Death of 1348-49 resulted in a shortage of labour, skilled and unskilled, and probably affected the building of the church which was under construction at that time. The labour shortage, the Statute of Labourers of 1351 which restricted the wages of many workers to what they had been before the Black Death, the Poll Taxes and the feudal conditions under which the peasants lived were all factors leading to the Peasants' Revolt in 1381. The local peasants rebelled under the leadership of Geoffrey Litester, a dyer of Felmingham, and marched to Norwich, where Litester assumed the title of 'King of the Commons' and forced important citizens to act as his servants. Pursued by Henry Despenser, the 'warlike' Bishop of Norwich, and his army, the rebels fled to North Walsham and erected barricades on the heath to the south of the town. They were defeated in a bitter struggle and after summary trial by the Bishop, Litester was sentenced to be hanged, drawn and quartered.

The fifteenth century saw the rise of the Paston family who lived in the village of Paston, five miles north-east of North Walsham. Clement Paston, a small landholder, borrowed money to send his son, William, to school. William profited by his education, became a lawyer and was made one of the justices of the Court of Common Pleas. His descendants were made Earls of Yarmouth in the seventeenth century. The Pastons are famous for their family letters of which over a thousand survive from about 1420 until 1627, providing an interesting insight into people's lives in those times. It was a member of this family, another William, who founded a Free School for Boys, later to be known as The Paston School, in 1606, in the centre of the town on a site which became available for the building after the disastrous fire of 1600.

The Churchwardens' Books contain a description of the event and the great damage it did, burning fiercely for two hours and destroying 'the wholle bodye of the towne, beinge built cheefly aboute the market place'. The church was fired in five places, but was not seriously damaged. The loss to the town was estimated at twenty thousand pounds and an appeal was made to the Queen's Council for wood for rebuilding 'because this part of the country is barren of timber'.

It was mainly the woollen industry which accounted for the growth and prosperity of North Walsham and its neighbourhood during the fourteenth and fifteenth centuries and for the building of its large parish church. The woollen industry continued to prosper until the eighteenth century and the Industrial Revolution, when Yorkshire with its mineral resources and water power took over the manufacture of woollen cloth.

When the nation was preparing to meet the threat of invasion by the Spaniards and their Armada, the churchwardens recorded the delivery of six hundred steel corselets for the Town Armour.

The nearness of North Walsham to the coast enabled some of its inhabitants to participate in smuggling in the eighteenth century, and, on one occasion, in July 1736, Customs Officers seized fourteen gallons of brandy and ninety pounds of tea in the town.

Situated as it is in an agricultural area, agriculture, and its accompanying occupations, has played a large part in the employment of the inhabitants. One firm in the town manufactured agricultural implements, such as ploughs, while others were engaged in the corn business, and one firm, which can trace its history back through many centuries, were reed thatchers, working as far afield as the United States of America. Another family founded a firm which made furniture which was supplied to London businesses and made the claim that no wood that had not been seasoned for sixteen years was used in their products.

Between the World Wars, North Walsham developed industrially, and, in more recent times, heavy engineering, the welding of plastics, the growing and canning of fruit and vegetables have provided employment. During the Second World War, a great amount of produce was canned in the town for shipment to the Forces serving in the most important battle areas in the world.

Many of the postcards used to illustrate this book were the work of photographers who lived in North Walsham.

Herbert S. Church is mentioned in a directory for 1908 as a photographer with a business in King's Arms Street and at Overstrand, a coastal village about eight miles north-east of the town. Presumably, his stay in North Walsham was short as the 1912 directory shows him at Overstrand only.

The name of Ralph Michael Ling appears on many postcards and he is mentioned in directories from 1908-1937 (the last Kelly's Directory), usually as a chemist, but on two occasions (1908 and 1925) as an optician and dealer in photographic materials.

George McLean is first mentioned in Harrod's Directory for 1877 as a photographer and proprietor of a fancy goods repository. In 1883, the photography business was continued by James McLean, in 1890 by Mrs. Jane McLean and in 1896 by the Misses Blanche and Mildred McLean. In 1900, Lawrence George McLean had a studio on the corner of King's Arms Street and Park Lane. From 1933 he appears only as a mineral water manufacturer.

The photographer, Francis Edward Long, is first mentioned in the North Walsham directories in 1922 as a tobacconist and his shop was on the corner of the Market Place and Church Street.

Market Cross, North Walsham

1. The market cross is the undisputed symbol of North Walsham and was built in the middle of the sixteenth century by Thomas Thirlby, the Bishop of Norwich and Lord of the Manor of North Walsham. It was destroyed in 1600 by the 'Great Fire of North Walsham' and rebuilt by Bishop Redman shortly afterwards. It first became known as the 'Town Clock' in 1787 when John Juler, a North Walsham watchmaker, fitted a clock from Worstead Hall.

Market Place, North Walsham

2. This Thursday scene shows the market about 1919, still with an unmetalled surface. Originally, the Market Place was the Lord of the Manor's demesne (home farm) and included a windmill. The prosperity brought by the Flemish weavers made it more profitable to rent out the land for market stalls, which eventually became the shops of today and many have frontages which are multiples of a seven-foot mediaeval stall.

3. This postcard shows the western approach to the town about 1910. On the left is the branch store of the Norwich Co-operative Society which opened in 1906. The building was commandeered by the military in 1915 and burned down in 1916. Rebuilt and opened in 1921, it continued trading until 1983 when it was closed.

4. Unfortunately, no details are known of this coach party standing before The Angel Hotel. It was in this hotel that George Edwards (later Sir George Edwards) founded The Eastern Counties Agricultural Labourers' and Smallholders' Union on July 6th, 1906, which later became known as The Agricultural Workers' Union. The Angel has been an hotel or inn for over two hundred years and its name was adopted by the North Walsham Football Club, which, founded in 1897, is the oldest amateur club in Norfolk.

5. This photograph, taken late during the First World War, is thought to be of a recruiting drive in the Market Place. The aeroplane, guarded by the soldier with fixed bayonet, is a Sopwith Pup, capable of 111 miles per hour. It was generally recognised as the most perfect flying-machine of World War I and was introduced in the summer of 1916.

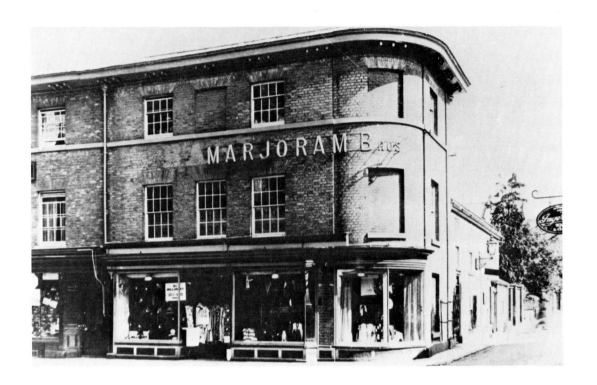

6. The first mention of Marjoram Brothers' Drapery Store at the end of Church Street was in directories of 1912. By 1933, the premises had become Brenners Penny Bazaar, then, in 1937, Peacocks Stores, followed by Woolworths, and in 1983, it assumed its present name of 'The Paper Shop'. Whatever the name, it provides an imposing façade at the eastern exit of the Market Place.

Market Place and Church, North Walsham

7. This card, with its high-level view, is postmarked 1908 and was taken from the top floor of Marjoram's Store. It clearly shows the narrowness of the shops on the north side of the Market Place which developed from mediaeval stalls placed on the frontage of the churchyard in an area known as 'Foreland'.

8. Horace Mace and Sons were well known cabinet makers, upholsterers and bedding manufacturers and proudly boasted that they were established in 1790. In 1927 they advertised high grade furniture at 'prices that are as low as is compatible with first rate material and workmanship'.

9. To celebrate the Coronation of King George V and Queen Mary on June 22nd, 1911, a dinner was given for 3,100 people, on 57 tables arranged in the Market Place. The meal included 213 stone of beef and 78 stone of puddings made to the recipe used for the Queen Victoria Diamond Jubilee in 1887. The day continued with children's sports, an evening carnival and concluded with the National Anthem and cheers for the King.

10. The Coronation Dinner of 1911 was organised in only eight weeks under the chairmanship of John Dixon (second from the right), auctioneer and chairman of the Town Council. The deficiencies in tables, seats and trestles were made up by the volunteer Trestle Brigade led by Fred Vincent. They are pictured at John Dixon's Tudor House in Grammar School Road with some of the 135 trestles made.

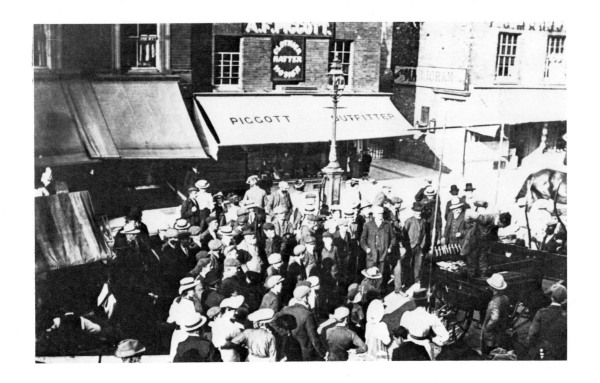

11. This animated view of the Market Place shows an attentive audience watching an escapologist practising his art on the back of a cart. The trestle and stall on the left suggest this was a Thursday market day which has been a part of the life of the town from time immemorial.

12. This photograph shows Mr. Fred Randell in front of his ironmongery shop in the Market Place. It was taken some time before 1897 when the shop was rebuilt. The business was founded in 1820 and their Northrepps foundry moved to Bacton Road, North Walsham, in 1865. The pig iron for the foundry was transported up the North Walsham-Dilham canal and then carted from Swafield Wharf. The new 1897 shop was one of the first in the district to be lit by electricity.

13. For a number of years this old Newsham fire engine was on display beneath the Market Cross as seen on this card. The engine was mentioned in the churchwardens' accounts about 1736 together with a description of the method of working it and its care. It has been restored and now has a safer home in the town's fire station.

14. This view of Starling's garage was taken about 1905. Situated conveniently on the road leading to the Norwich Turnpike, it served the few cars then travelling the untarred roads. Petroleum spirit had been available in North Walsham since 1902. The business still thrives but is now concerned with coach hire and motor cycle sales.

15. North Walsham's volunteer Fire Brigade was formed in February, 1883, and purchased an engine capable of throwing 100 gallons of water 100 feet high each minute. With the passage of time, progress was made, and this crew's pride in their modern fire engine of 1921 is self-evident. Standing before the engine are (left to right): W.A. Griston (Lieutenant), Albert Walker (Captain) and Harry Walker (Lieutenant).

16. This photograph of the second motor fire engine in action at the west end of the Market Place is thought to have been taken at the time of a fire in The Butchery in the 1920's. In the background is Philip Griston's chemist's and optician's shop. Phil Griston was the son of Lieutenant W.A. Griston on the previous photograph and was in business until he retired in 1964.

17. Norfolk has a long history of thatching because of the ready availability of good quality reed in the area. The Farman family have been thatchers for many centuries and have earned Royal Patronage. The business moved to North Walsham in 1880 at the Garden House, Aylsham Road, a site carefully chosen for its proximity to a town pump as a ready supply of water was necessary to soak the willows used in basketwork in which the firm was also engaged.

18. The 'Town' station was opened on October 20th, 1874, with a processional arch and celebrations on the Station Field opposite. This picture of the smartly uniformed staff was taken about 1920 when the station was still the junction for the Mundesley Branch Line, which opened in 1898. In 1923 the junction was transferred to the 'Main' station.

19. This photograph, taken about 1910, shows the derailment of the Overstrand train at the North Walsham Great Eastern Station, later the 'Main' station, which occurred while it was shunting between platforms prior to departure. Overstrand was the limit of operation for Great Eastern trains on the Norfolk and Suffolk Committee's joint line extension between Mundesley and Cromer. At this time, there was fierce rivalry with the Midland and Great Northern Railway and their North Walsham 'Town' station.

28560 North Walsham. Grammar School Road.

20. The name Grammar School Road, formerly Free School Road, is taken from the main entrance to the Paston School. On Thursdays, this could be a dangerous road to travel as herds of cattle were driven down it from the cattle market on Yarmouth Road to the railway station on Norwich Road. The buildings on the left were part of The Bull Inn, which no longer exists.

21. This rare postcard of Grammar School Road shows two buskers, a man with a violin and a woman with a harp, performing to a small but attentive audience. The site on the left has been for many years the home of local builders, from Robert Cornish in the 1850's to William Bird and Son Contractors of today.

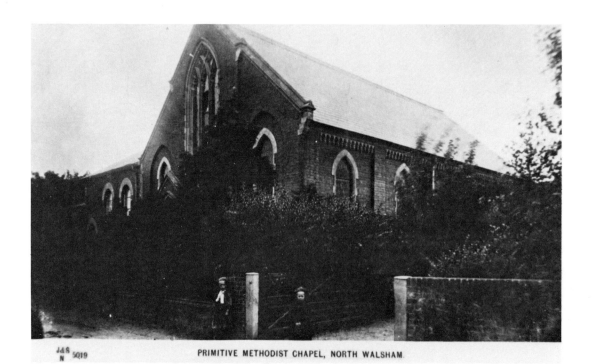

PRIMITIVE METHODIST CHAPEL, NORTH WALSHAM.

22. Built in 1890 on Grammar School Road, this chapel replaced the Primitive Methodist chapel in Hall Lane, which became the George Edwards Memorial Hall and is now occupied by a firm of printers. In 1934, the Primitive and the Wesleyan Methodists united and the name changed to the Methodist Church. The part on the left has been rebuilt as a hall and is the venue of the Methodist Sunday School.

NORTH WALSHAM GRAMMAR SCHOOL

23. The Paston School was founded by Sir William Paston in 1606 on land bought from Robert Chawner following the Great Fire of North Walsham in 1600. The present school house was built in 1765 on the site of the original house built about 1604. This card is a copy of John Berney Ladbrooke's lithograph of 1827 and bears the Paston coat of arms and motto in old French of which the translation is 'From good to better everywhere'.

North Walsham Paston Grammar School (Nelson's School)

24. This view was taken about 1920 and autographed by George Hare who was headmaster from 1904 until 1922. His appointment was a break with tradition as he was neither clergyman nor graduate. Under his headship the number of pupils rose from 30 to 220. Horatio Nelson attended the school from 1769 to 1771 before leaving to join his first ship, the 'Raisonnable'. In 1984, the school became the Paston Sixth Form College.

North Walsham Church

25. The Church of St. Nicholas incorporates part of the tower of an older church dating from the tenth or eleventh century. The building of the 'new' church began about 1330 and work was interrupted in 1348 when the 'Black Death' is thought to have caused a lack of skilled masons. The tower was originally 147 feet high but falls in 1724, 1836, and the removal of dangerous portions reduced it to its present form.

North Walsham Church.

26. This view, from the south-east, shows the size of the church to its best advantage. It is 156 feet long and almost 70 feet wide. The great east window was blown in by a gale in 1809. The present elaborate tracery of the window dates from 1874 when Sir William Forster provided for its restoration.

ANCIENT. ALTAR. TABLE. N. WALSHAM. CHURCH.   LINCE. SERIES. 14.

27. The inscription on this finely carved altar table reads:
AND BLOOD
THE BODY OF OVR LORD JESVS CHRIST WAS GEVEN FOR THE
PRESERVE THY BODY AND SOVLE VNTO EVERLASTING LYFE. AMEN.
The addition of the words 'and blood' at a later date, suggest the table was made between the first and second Prayer Books of Edward VI, namely between 1549 and 1552 when orders were issued that stone altars should be destroyed and wooden tables substituted.

THE OLD CHEST. N. WALSHAM CHURCH

28. Within the church can still be seen this chest or hutch, bound and studded with iron. It dates from the times when the organisation of the town was undertaken by church-appointed officials and was the repository for church valuables and papers relating to the guilds and the parish generally. The seven locks ensured that seven witnesses attended its every opening.

29. After founding his school, Sir William Paston made arrangements with John Key, a freemason of London, for the erection of his tomb in the Parish Church at a cost of £200. Central in its design is Sir William's effigy 'in armor, resting upon his arme, of five foot and a half longe in allabaster'. Sir William died in October, 1610, just two years after its completion. It was intended to bring the body of his wife, Frances, from Paston village to join him, but, apparently, the body of Mary Paston, wife of Erasmus Paston, was disinterred and brought in error.

SIR W. PASTON'S TOMB   LING'S SERIES 20

THE.OAKS.NORTH.WALSHAM.   LING'S SERIES.

30. The Oaks, North Walsham's finest mansion, was demolished in the 1930's and the site is now occupied by the Post Office. The estate was formerly a possession of the Withers family until their heiress took it to the Coopers on her marriage to Thomas Cooper of Yarmouth in 1760, where it remained for three generations. Latterly, it became the home of the Wilkinson family.

31. The 'New' Road, which has just passed its bicentenary, owes its construction to Thomas Cooper, who lived at The Oaks. It was built behind his mansion to replace the old Happisburgh Road, which bisected the Cooper estate, so that Old Captain Cooper, as he was better known, could lay out his improved park.

32. This old house stood in Ship Yard and is believed to have been a weaver's house because of the width of the first-floor window, a feature that can be seen on a number of other buildings in the town, including The Feathers Hotel. The house was demolished in the early 1970's to make way for a shopping precinct.

33. To the right of the cast iron town pump is The Cross Keys Hotel. Once part of The Oaks estate, it was already a public house in 1604 when Robert Watts received a licence to keep an ale house there. It had its heyday at the turn of the century when a cattle market thrived behind it. The decline and closure of the cattle market, built on its bowling green, led in turn to its closure in the 1970's. Its façade is substantially retained as the frontage to Woolworth's store.

34. Taken shortly after 1906, this postcard shows 'Bruff' Hewitt and Dan Mount at the town pump collecting water to flush out the drainage channels. The pump was said to be connected with the only well which never ran dry, but an enquiry into a new water works found that this well, and most wells in the town, had water which was unfit for human consumption.

35. Dan Mount is shown completing his work of flushing the channels. The town drainage system consisted of such open channels which, connected to a brick sewer, led down Gas Works Loke to the small stream called the Town Drain. This stream flowed north from Northfield Road, formerly Catchpit Lane, to the river at Swafield.

36. In 1901, Major H.A. Barclay of Hanworth Hall was selected to raise the King's Own Royal Regiment of Norfolk Imperial Yeomanry. North Walsham was the centre for Squadron B of the Regiment and the Squadron is pictured above, parading in the Market Place. In November 1902, the Regiment provided the escort for the visit of the Emperor of Germany to Sandringham.

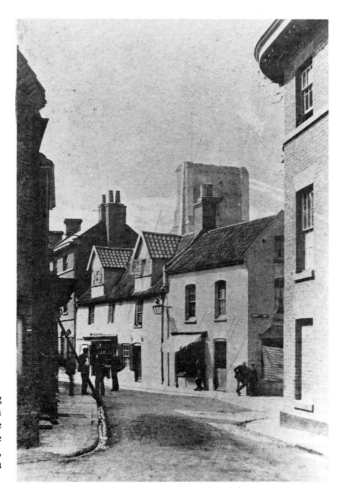

37. North Walsham was once described as being *'Long' at each end and 'Miles' in the middle* from the names of the shopkeepers that were in the town. This pre-1920 view of the eastern end of the Market Place shows shops owned by Anne Long, which have now become clothes shops and a Chinese food Take-away.

38. Immediately east of the church wall is Church Street — previously named Swan Street and Buck Street after inns which were sited there. Whilst the shop on the right is still a grocer's, the son, Mr. E.B. LeGrice, started a nursery business in 1920 and reached considerable fame in rose hybridisation, producing seventy-five commercial varieties. The White Swan, which was built in 1636, is still an inn.

39. The Wesleyan Methodists began a North Walsham Circuit in 1813. This chapel, on the corner of Church Street and Hall Lane, was built in 1820 and remained in use until about 1934 when the Wesleyans united with the Primitive Methodists. The building is now occupied by shops, but the first floor windows still indicate its former use.

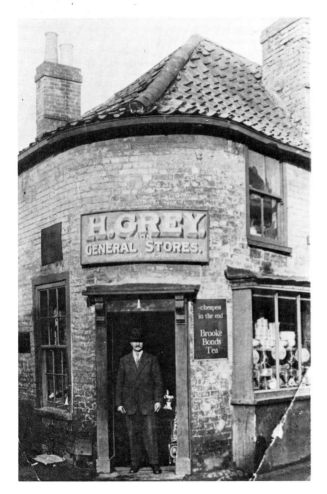

40. This building was The Rose and Crown Inn before it became Mr. Grey's shop and stood at the corner of Bacton Road and Back Street. In his 'General Stores', Mr. Grey sold almost everything from wall-paper to paraffin, from flour to tobacco. This is another of our lost buildings and the site is now at the edge of the Vicarage Street car park.

41. This photograph of 1930-31 is a tantalising reminder of the prices of yesteryear. The garage business was started by Edward Hannant in 1928 on its present, expanded, Bacton Road site. Edward was joined by his brothers, Leslie and Walter, who were, initially and respectively, a carpenter and a thatcher. The business still thrives under the control of the sons of Edward and Walter.

THE MONUMENT, NORTH WALSHAM

42. A mile south of the town is a fourteenth century cross, one of three, which reputedly mark the site where Henry Despenser, Bishop of Norwich, defeated the Norfolk rising of the Peasants' Revolt of 1381. The rising was against taxation and enforced feudal labour and the peasants' leader, Geoffrey Litester, was captured, hanged and quartered.

43. Stump Cross is the northernmost of the three crosses mentioned on the previous page. The cross was removed by Thomas Cooper and coins found beneath it were given to a Yarmouth museum. By 1930 it was almost buried and Mr. C.W. Barritt, Chairman of the Urban District Council, remounted it on a concrete base as seen in this picture.

44. North Walsham's premier building firm, Cornish and Gaymer, began with Robinson Cornish, from Knapton, who was listed in 1858 as a builder and ecclesiastical carver. About 1877 he joined forces with John Gaymer and there is much evidence in the town of their excellent work. The Mason's shop seen here was situated on Millfield on an area now occupied by H.P. Foods Ltd.

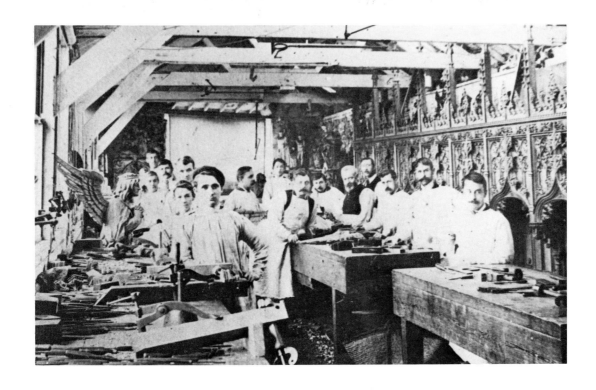

45. Cornish and Gaymer's Joiners' shop, also at Millfield, was situated beside the railway. Their most famous carver was Charles Henry Simpson, who was born at North Walsham in 1856. His first piece of work, when he was sixteen years old, was the carving on the altar of the Parish Church. Other examples of his work are to be found in Norwich Cathedral, Durham Cathedral, Winchester College Chapel, the crucifix in the grounds of the Roman Catholic Church at North Walsham and a host of other Norfolk and Norwich churches.

Catholic Church of the Sacred Heart of Jesus, Market Place, North Walsham.

✠

SUNDAYS—

Mass, 9 30 a.m. (and Sermon)

Benediction, 6 30 p.m. (and Sermon)

WEEK-DAYS—

Mass, 8 a.m.

Confessions—

Before Mass (and as notified in the Church).

46. In 1904, a small congregation first gathered in a chapel on the upper floor of Mr. Frank Loads' business premises near the Market Cross in North Walsham to hear the Catholic Mass. This chapel, pictured in this unusual postcard, continued to be used until 1935 when a permanent building was erected in the grounds of Mr. Loads' private house on the Norwich Road.

King's Arms Street, North Walsham

47. The view on this card is now much altered. The Bull Inn was demolished in 1970 to make way for road improvements and a mini-roundabout. The trees on the left were removed to allow for the building of the Catholic Church in 1935.

CATHOLIC CHURCH OF THE SACRED HEART, NORTH WALSHAM

48. In 1935, the Catholic Church was built in King's Arms Street by Cornish and Gaymer. In the main, it was erected as the gift of Mr. Frank Loads and his first wife, Sarah Monica Loads, and partly that of Mrs. Lawrence Hudson. Inside, the Stations of the Cross are striking, and in one of the side chapels, there is a fine statue of St. Nicholas, the patron saint of sailors and children.

49. Named after an hotel of that name, this part of King's Arms Street retains much of its original character. The fine flint and brick gabled building was an extension built by Cornish and Gaymer. It housed the North Walsham telephone exchange for a number of years and is now the premises of a firm of solicitors.

THE PICTUREDROME

**King's Arms Street
North Walsham**

—

Manager : H. P. Coates.

—

Latest and Best Talking Pictures

Always a good show. Ask Our Patrons.

**Monday to Friday Nightly at 7.30.
Saturday Night continuous from 6.30.**

Admission 1/6, 1/-, 9d. and 6d.

Best seats bookable—no extra charge. **Entire Change of Pictures Mondays and Thursdays.** Support your Theatre and get into the habit of at least one visit per week. The better the Theatre is patronised the Greater the Attractions

50. This, the town's first cinema, was built by Mr. Nixon in 1912 and later taken over by Mr. John Dixon. It lasted until September 1931 when it was forced to close just one week after the opening of the Regal Cinema on New Road. The circular gable can still be seen in King's Arms Street where the building now houses a carpet shop.

51. In March 1918 an army cadet force was formed at the Paston Grammar School during the headship of George Hare. In this postcard of 1925 the Corps is pictured marching past The Bull Inn towards the school's playing field on the Norwich Road.

52. This fine early postcard looks back down the Cromer Road — previously named Antingham Lane — to the western exit of the town. The small thatched and dormerroofed cottages have made way for the car park of The Angel Hotel, but, otherwise, the scene has altered little over the years.

53. North Walsham has a long history of Nonconformity. The Congregationalists formed their first permanent church in a barn in Bradfield. In North Walsham a chapel was built in Vicarage Street in 1809 and this Neo-Gothic style church was built on the Cromer Road in 1857 for £1,200 and a new organ was added in 1883 for a further £250.

NORTH WALSHAM STEAM LAUNDRY Cᵒ Lᵀᴰ
DYERS AND DRY CLEANERS

54. This postcard of the North Walsham Steam Laundry, with its Straker Squire van parked beside it, was taken about 1920. Established in 1900, the company advertised in 1904 as laundrymen, dyers and french cleaners. It survived a fire in 1906 to become one of the foremost laundries in East Anglia. A by-pass runs along the railway where the photographer stood and the quiet fields to the right have become a busy industrial estate.

MUNDSLEY ROAD. N. WALSHAM   LING'S SERIES

55. This view of about 1910 was taken beside the cemetery wall. Formerly named Swafield Lane, Mundesley Road has several historical connections. In the eighteenth century the workhouse was on this road. In 1877, at 'Kyneton', the Misses Cooke started their school for girls. In the 1890's the Continental Relay Station was built, receiving three cables from the shore at Bacton and one from Mundesley. Also, during World War I, 'Wellingtonia' was a Red Cross Hospital.

56. The Board School, as it was originally known, opened in 1874 and was built by Mr. R. Cornish of North Walsham. Designed for 230 boys, 180 girls and 200 infants, it was one of the 'Penny Schools' where each of the children had to pay a penny per week and provide their own stationery. It now forms part of a larger Primary School.

57. This view of the school is from Hall Lane and is now largely obscured by houses. Opposite the school is a crossroads: Marshgate, to the left, led to low-lying grazing land, and, to the right, is Pound Road on which stood the cattle pound where strays were impounded until they were claimed.

BACTON WOOD MILL, NORTH WALSHAM 16

58. Built beside the River Ant and near the meeting of the boundaries of four parishes, this mill has been a frequent source of dispute. It is mentioned several times in the fifteenth century Paston Letters, usually in connection with cases of trespass. In the nineteenth century there was a further dispute as to which parish should bury a man who died in the mill. The mill was kept by William Wells (1836), William Burton (1854) and Edward Press (1883). It is now a private dwelling.

59. This view of 1912 shows wherries on the North Walsham-Dilham Canal at Bacton Wood Bridge. The canal ran from Antingham Ponds to Wayford Bridge and was opened in 1826. It used fourteen ton wherries, but so small was the flow that only three wherries a day could sail in either direction. As more economical forms of transport developed, the canal declined and the last regular wherry reached Ebridge Mill in 1935.

60. Ebridge Mill, photographed here about 1930, is thought to be one of the two North Walsham mills mentioned in Domesday Book and was called Everbupes Watermill in Henry VIII's reign. When the North Walsham-Dilham Canal opened, it received the first delivery by wherry, watched by 'thousands of spectators', shortly before the official opening in 1826. Although water power is no longer used, the mill supports a thriving business to this day.

61. The arrival of the first twenty ton Scammell lorry at Ebridge Mills was the occasion when this picture was taken. In the background is the mill's own Napier lorry, the bodywork of which was made by Frank Mann in his works in Vicarage Street.

39236. NORTH WALSHAM: YARMOUTH ROAD.

62. This scene, looking north towards the town, appears on a number of postcards which show its progressive development as pavements replace footpaths and wooden fences replace the grassy banks on the left. On the right is The Oaks estate, on the left were several better class houses, including The Limes which was leased to the Paston School in 1912 when its boarding population reached one hundred.

63. This postcard shows a procession approaching the town centre along the Yarmouth Road. The wall of The Oaks estate, built by prisoners held during the Napoleonic War, has gone and the land behind it is now the site of a post office, a telephone exchange and a garage. To the right of the picture, the buildings and cattle market have been replaced by a supermarket.

POLICE STATION, NORTH WALSHAM.

64. Built in 1903, pictured in 1914, this County Police Station, County Court and Petty Sessional Court House replaced the former Police Station in Vicarage Street where Superintendent Lovick had two constables to assist him and two cells in which to keep prisoners. In 1971, the building on the left was demolished to make way for an enlarged Police Station.

65. This is Youngman's Mill at the turn of the century. It was sited off the Yarmouth Road near the farm buildings which still remain at the entrance to Thirlby Road. The conventional Norfolk post mill with its red brick roundhouse was named after the Youngman milling family and ceased working shortly after 1890. It was demolished in 1902.

War Memorial Cottage Hospital, North Walsham.

66. The hospital was built in 1923 as a memorial to the 179 men from North Walsham and district who gave their lives in the 1914-1918 Great War. It was built at a cost of £4,366 on a one-acre site given by Mrs. John Wilkinson. The foundation stone was laid by Lady Suffield, and it was opened in August 1924 by H.R.H. Princess Marie Louise.

The Elms School, North Walsham.

67. The Elms School was the name that the Misses Cooke took from their North Street School when they moved to The Lawns in 1905. The building on the left was added in 1909. The centre block is all that remains of the original Scarburgh House, built by Henry Scarburgh shortly after the Great Fire of 1600. It became The Girls' High School and will form a part of the Paston Sixth Form College in 1984.

High Street, North Walsham

68. Although this postcard bears the title 'High Street', it is in fact Market Street, North Walsham. The opening on the right leads to Old Bear Yard. The buildings on the left were originally Three Feathers Row, which led down to Scarburgh or Kendall's House, now part of the Girl's High School. Maurice Kendall married Mary, the Scarburgh heiress, whose family is also remembered by Scarborough Hill and House on the Yarmouth Road.

Market Street, North Walsham.

69. This is a fine reminder of North Walsham early in the present century with its open drain running down the right of the street. The irregular collection of buildings in front of the church evolved from the mediaeval flesh market, later called The Butchery. On the right, in front of The Feathers Hotel, were the town stocks.

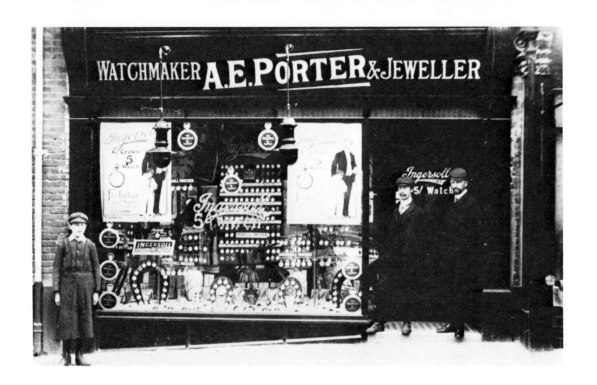

70. This photograph, taken about 1910 by R.M. Ling, is of Mr. Porter's shop in Market Street. The property is now a newsagent's, the jewellery business having moved to the Market Place where, in 1928, it was taken over by Mr. L.F. Hancock and, subsequently, in 1978 by Mr. M.R. Bell.

71. Their first motor ambulance provides the back-drop for the North Walsham Division of the St. John Ambulance Brigade in 1924. Central in the group are Mr. G.B. Fuller, Superintendent for thirty-one years, Dr. C.H.W. Page, who was largely responsible for the Division's formation, and Mr. John Dixon, President for fourteen years until his death in 1938.

72. Furze Hill, on the Happisburgh Road, was built in 1896 by Mrs. Petre, widow of Lieutenant Colonel James Duff. She assumed the surname of her uncle, John Berney Petre, after his death in 1881. Resigning Westwick House to her elder son, she took her other children, Granville, Lilian and Mildred, to Furze Hill. The Duffs were strong supporters of the Salvation Army and, eventually, Mildred left Furze Hill to the Salvation Army and it has become their Eventide Home for the elderly.

73. These two hexagonal houses on the Norwich Road were built about 1814 by John Berney Petre as a toll gate, replacing the original toll gate at Monument Cottage on the North Walsham-Norwich Turnpike. Both houses are still extant and occupied in spite of being situated on a stretch of road reputedly haunted by the ghost of a suicide who hanged himself in the nearby woods.

Westwick Pond,
nr. North Walsham

74. This often photographed 'Captain's Pond' was constructed on the Westwick estate by John Berney Petre in the 1770's. The name is thought to refer to Captain William Varlo who married Petre's daughter and then assumed the name of Petre. Westwick possessed a renowned duck decoy which was probably on this lake. Lying beside the Norwich Road, the Pond has changed little since 1915 when this picture was taken.

75. This peaceful Edwardian scene was transformed on Sundays when the people of North Walsham took their regular Sunday afternoon walk. It is said that you had to make an early start if you wanted a seat on the post and rail fence near Captain's Pond. It was in this dip that William Cooper, a famous North Walsham coachman, overturned the 'Pilot' coach and was killed.

GATEWAY, WESTWICK,

76. This spectacular Westwick Arch was hurriedly demolished in September, 1981, amid fierce public protest. It was built about 1780 as part of John Berney Petre's medal-winning scheme at Westwick. Originally a flint-quoined and rendered dovecot, it was the entrance to Westwick House, the road to Norwich passing to the west. Later, it stood across the North Walsham to Norwich turnpike when the road was diverted about 1797.